BREATHING IN PORTUGUESE, LIVING IN ENGLISH

ALSO BY HEATHER TOSTESON

Germs of Truth

The Sanctity of the Moment: Poems from Four Decades

God Speaks My Language, Can You?

Hearts as Big as Fists & Other Stories

Visible Signs

BREATHING IN PORTUGUESE, LIVING IN ENGLISH

Heather Tosteson

Wising Up Press Collective
Wising Up Press
Decatur, Georgia

Wising Up Press
P.O. Box 2122
Decatur, GA 30031-2122
www.universaltable.org

Copyright © 2014 by Heather Tosteson

All rights reserved. No part of this book may be used or reproduced in any manner whatsoever without written permission, except in the case of brief quotations embodied in critical articles or reviews.

Catalogue-in-Publication data is on file with the Library of Congress.
LCCN: 2013957506

Wising Up ISBN: 978-0-9826933-1-5

DEDICATION

A minha raposa manhosa,
I miss you . . .

Breathing in Portuguese, Living in English

The Beginning	*O começo*	*1*

A concatenação

Concatenation	*A concatenação*	*4*
U-Turn	*Voltando-se*	*5*
Stubborn Age	*A velhice turrona*	*6*
A Mortal Knot	*Um nó mortal*	*7*
Unusual Tranquility	*A tranquilidade descomunal*	*8*
A Step	*Um passo*	*9*
Spare Change	*O troco*	*10*
To Put it Simply	*Trocar em miúdos*	*12*
Hurry Up	*Rápido*	*13*

As verdades

Home Truths	*As verdades*	*16*
Doing Without Language	*Prescindindo da língua*	*17*
Empty	*Vão ou vazio*	*18*
Frames of Reference	*Nossos arcabouços*	*20*
The Destination	*O destino*	*23*

Recompor

Dead Ahead	*Em frente*	*26*
Pining	*A saudade*	*27*
A Breech	*Uma brecha*	*32*
Reset	*Recompor*	*34*
Resplendent	*Resplandecente*	*37*

No meio deste

In the Thick of This	*No meio deste*	*40*
Supported	*Apoiou*	*42*
Longings and Belongings	*Os anseios e os pertences*	*44*
Abandoning Assumptions	*Abandonando as suposições*	*46*
Belongings	*Os haveres*	*49*
In Full Strength, Overwhelmingly	*Na marra*	*50*
Complete, Utter, Ultimate	*Cabal*	*51*

Em casa

Home	*Em casa*	*56*
To Be at the Mercy of Cicadas and Compassion	*Ficar a mercê das cigarras e da misericórdia*	*60*

O COMEÇO
THE BEGINNING

Eu começo—I begin
with a combination, *uma combinação
das línguas*, languages, such a shush
and churr of consonants and brown
skin and dreams of computer screens,
empty schema. *Praia da Joaquina,* Joaquina Beach,
Lagoa da Conceição, Lake of Conception,
and another lake of concepts, *lagoa de concepções
cheia de queixas de casais,* full, too full,
of those fractious quibbles unique to any couple,
everywhere you turn, rippling, glinting . . .
I just don't know,
hoje, ontem ou amanhã,
today, yesterday or whatever follows,
how to live *uma vida,*
this one, mine, with its limited
mileage, *quilometragem limitada,
imprescindível,* so unpredictable,
ardente, vulnerável,
and pure.

A CONCATENAÇÃO

CONCATENATION

A CONCATENAÇÃO
CONCATENATION

Concatenation, one sound
toppling after another into sense.
But this transposition—R to H—
stymies my mind every time.
My eye recognizes.
Reanimar.
Realmente.
My ear rejects.
HAYanimah
HAYowmenchee

But surely curiosity revives,
at whatever age, one word,
reanimar, after another, *realmente.*
And then we feel the sharp tug, slow give
of Pandora's box, and there it is—
so much life ready to wing it.
Why do I catch my breath, not sing it?
Reanimar.
Realmente.

Cada língua concebe outro eu,
every language conceives another I,
igualmente essencial, new.

Voltando-se
U-Turn

Our first days here we spent so much
time pretending our habits would hold,
we almost missed our new world.
Sôfrega, avid, for the old,
and *igualmente sôfrega* for the footprint
we have yet to make, *profundar*
with our full weight, *e desocupar,*
empty, *outra vez.*

How many times, in how many places,
do we have to learn there's nothing
to hold onto, so no reason
to hold back? *Uma e outra vez,*
again and again we put to good use,
aproveitamos, this truth
tão rude e forte, so crude
and strong: *Ir toda vida reto*
é igual a dar uma volta,
to forge on is equal
to doing an about face,
in a world round and fat
as the belly, *a barriga,*
de Buddha,
or a woman fulfilling, *grávida,*
tão grávida, her term,
or the universe turning back at last
to hold us fast.

A velhice turrona
Stubborn Age

Mamamos o mamão, we suckle on papaya,
and in our dreams we nurse at *velhice,* age,
like something primeval and innocent.
A velhice tastes sweet as the universe
expanding inside us
and acrid as a burnt match,
an afterthought. So many words
we have lost *e mais, mais,* more, more,
than we can *imaginar ou gostar,*
imagine or taste, still await us,
nos esperam—like life itself,
teaching us each second
infinity's melodious
o compasso, measure.

Um nó mortal
A Mortal Knot

Eu não sei se estou, I don't know if I am
making or unmaking, *fazendo o desfazendo
esse nó,* this knot, *tão intricado,*
so intricate and intransigent.
For months it has weighed in heavily
just there under my sternum—
uma coisa terrível, a terrible thing, inescapable.
Like black glass annealed by the wildfire
of my own fear, it gleams unseen
deep in the darkness that is me
anywhere and everywhere I go.
Meu nó. My knot. *Só meu.*
Only mine. *Inevitável.*
Inescapable. And maybe deadly.

In Portuguese *mortal* means
mortal and dreadful and perhaps
that's exactly what I've come here
to *desfazer* or just wrap myself around
like an old woman centuries ago carried
the knowledge that at the heart of her swam
an embryo turned to stone—
and she herself lived, harbored
other life, birthed it, but this,
this, so *atrevida,* daring, so of her and so not,
broke free—and, blessedly, stayed.

A Tranquilidade Descomunal
Unusual Tranquility

Incomun, unusual,
mas uma norma nova, but a new norm,
algo que eu posso tocar, something I can touch
diariamente, daily, with my imagination
like skin, *a pele,* touches *a pele,*
like my own hand touches my own face
as I wake from sweet sleep
to the rustle of wind in tall stands of bamboo.

These days, *eu sonho,* I dream
of a subterranean stream of story
I can tap into, a sensuality forever
available, even at my age, especially
at my age, *desfazendo nada,* undoing nothing,
revisando nada, revising nothing,
tudo, everything, *nada,*
nothing, *o todo,* all.

Um passo
A Step

Why *have* we come?
Eu me achego à dúvida,
I cozy up to doubt like *uma pergunta,*
a question with only one answer,
one I'll never know—
like the morning light
on my own grave
the year after I've filled it.
Eu deixo as aproximações
I abandon the approximations
como uma santa deixa seus sonhos de sexo,
as a saint abandons dreams of sex,
and the adolescent jettisons sanctity.
I reject, *eu veto,* the has been and could be
and wait—*completamente sossegada,*
quiet, approachable and
aventurosa, adventuresome.

O troco
Spare Change

i
Is there ever any spare change? Or is it always
necessary—and fat with chance?
A troco de que ela fez isso?
Why on earth did she do that?
A troco de que eu faço neste momento—
and why on earth do I at this moment do
something so ridiculously, redemptively simple,
like opening a door into another hemisphere
and walking carelessly through it.

ii
A hummingbird rests motionless on a mimosa branch,
its chest glowing, a giddy green, then shivers
into motion, hovers and thrusts greedily
into the throats of closed hibiscus.
The wind wavers but the butterflies, *as borboletas,*
delicately *determinadas,* ride its careless shifts
hither and yon until they find me.

iii
Three days ago in a bedroom shadowed
by bamboo and mango, I spoke with my dearest friend,
the holder of my story with all its sharp turns,
its fierce will, *sua vontade feroz*
e sua ternura atrevida, foolhardy tenderness,
and doubts, ah, those doubts, *as dúvidas*
claras e leves, clear and buoyant as this light.

And she heard me, as steadfast
a holder of my small changes as I am
of hers—whatever language I'm living in
this month, this year. Whatever hemisphere.

iv
And I too, in turn, listened. I drank it all in,
the small twists and turns of her daily life:
the silent son with the constructive soul of an architect,
the eloquence of his latest edifice, the sister-in-law
who after six months still won't trust
her baby to water's caress. Only later,
our connection broken, *tive um troço*,
as I realized with a shock that at the very same time
I was listening so intently to her, my mind
had expanded *simultâneamente no sonho*
into dream, and I, fearless, *existi e desenvolvi*,
lived for hours in this strange dual consciousness
that was too long for stroke or seizure, too short
for transformation. *O meu troco espiritual.*
My spare change of the spirit. *E também*
and also, *o meu troço espiritual*, my spiritual pang.
My, *meu*, spare, shocking change—as always,
haphazard, evanescent, and as real
and as slipshod as its consequences.

Trocar em miúdos
To Put It Simply

Ainda não, ainda bem, ainda por cima.
Not yet, just as well, and on top of that,
espichada on the beach, stretched out half asleep,
I woke into an understanding, *uma apercepção
conhecida, espantosa, e sossegada,*
familiar, astounding, and quiet, so very quiet.
Woke to something so *entranhado,*
bone deep, that to know it is to know myself
as just this: a distant island; an horizon
that underscores the difference
between these two equally true
blues; and an easy sweep
of green, mountainous coast
cradling the undrinkable.

The only response is to dance
the mute body, *o corpo
mudo, e ainda por cima,*
on top of that, to sing
the bewildered heart, *o coração
tão aturdido,*
and enter through this
uma síntese sensual, não-ficcional,
a true, sensuous synthesis,
in both languages.

RÁPIDO
Hurry Up

Hurry up in Spanish is *rápido!*
And here in Florionópolis it's happy do!
Rápido! Rápido! It's catching
and we take to chanting it with its hints
of a tune from South Pacific as our heels
slur up and down the dunes of the south Atlantic.
Rápido! Rápido! Happy view. Happy few.
Another *aula*, class, and our mantra modulates
to *rapidinho*. And our names for ourselves
in this, our *terceira idade*, old age, third stage,
soften too: *meu velhinho, minha velhinha,*
we murmur, *como está?* How *are* you
on this dusky, wind-thrumming afternoon in *Brasil?*
On the crest of the next dune, breathless
we pause, alight with *dúvidas*, doubts, but
aloft, like Daedalus, on something thicker, richer.
Do we use *tudo* or *todo*, we wonder,
no one to answer to but each other.
We shrug then, taking in the sureness
of our descent, the lift of this instant,
and just sing out *bem*
like a benediction.

AS VERDADES

HOME TRUTHS

As verdades
Home Truths

We bring our *as jeitos*, our little sleights of hand,
and *as verdades,* our home truths with us,
and no language somersaults us free
from our habits, *mortais e imortais*—like breathing
and bringing forth from depths forever
unknown to us gifts, *os presentes,*
rifts, *as fissuras,* grace notes,
and *o som sem a música,* sound
without music, *o som que dura,* sound that lasts
as pure hubbub, *o barulho puro,* such a tumult,
such a racket, that it brings God, our mother,
crooning to her knees to comfort us like babies
as we learn anew, *aprendemos de novo,*
the mystery *que vive em nossos olhos mudos,*
and lives in her eyes too, so similarly
mute and speaking—a pure charge
of existence, *silencioso, eterno, provocante,*
and immeasurable and wise
as fresh bread, broken
open.

Prescindindo da língua
Doing Without Language

Eu nunca escolho este estado, I never chose
this state, not in utero, not at birth,
sound the only amnion left to me.
Sucedeu, aconteceu, it happened, willy nilly,
without my willing. I became my sole source,
minha única fonte, spilling
a ânsia, anxiety, *a fúria,* rage, *a necessidade,* need,
and *o desejo,* desire, into the cool, desultory light.
Only my mother knew the truth and ruefully
named me, Heather, to civilize me,
to mute it, *ela,* this *a vida,*
so wordless, savage, *selvagem,*
resounding, and *redimida,*
redeemed.

VÃO OU VAZIO
EMPTY

i
They're both at this point just words
in a worn book, modifiers, descriptors,
adjectives with nothing—or everything—
to attach to. *Vão ou vazio,* which to choose?
Empty, vain, fruitless, unavailing, futile?
Or empty, void, bare, vacuous, unoccupied?
There's an openness to *vazio,*
a hint of commitment, however minimal,
to this language that swaddles almost all words
in *vogais,* vowels—words that in English
we prefer to bring, like *as vogais,* to a tidy close:
froo-**strah**-doo (*frustrado*), frustrated,
free-voh-loo (*frívolo*), frivolous,
in-**ooh**-tee-oo (*inútil*), useless,
ee-hay-**ow** (*irreal*), unreal
o **heep**-ee **hoh**-pee, hip hop
o **hoh**-kee an **hoh**-lee, rock and roll.

ii
How *vão* the simple sound: Hello.
But we miss it every day. We start,
then close our mouths around it, for
this is a culture that saves its smiles
for those they already know. Even so,
we feel at home somehow, *nossos motivos,*
our motives for coming here still intact,
but we, ourselves, *revirados,*
changed in ways we can't name.
We're the same and estranged,
stuffed to the gills with new words, old
desires, *os desejos velhos.* So we *descompomos*, muddle,
past and future, *a íntegra*, the whole, with our will,
tão vão, so empty, refulgent, still.

Nossos arcabouços
Frames of Reference

Eu não tenho muito em meu arcabouço,
I don't have much knowledge banked,
and what's there can't be shared.
These days, the armature itself feels rickety.
Or maybe, *talvez,* that's not true,
maybe it's all one aquifer—
that overflows when someone, somewhere,
stamps her foot in rage, *na raiva,* or surprise, *na surpresa.*
Or that gets tapped into when a diviner's rod quivers
carelessly in the cooling air and someone dares
to act on that *repercussão,* that repercussion.
Or that, salt with years, just swallows up
without warning, *sem aviso,* entire houses,
todo o trabalho duma vida, a life's work.

So, today, at *só* fifty-eight, surrounded by downpour,
a chuva, a chuva, a chuva, and Chopin, tapping in,
this is what spilled out from *meu arcabouço*:
Viver é fazer a cada idade
os erros catastróficos e casuais,
To live is to make at every age
catastrophic and random mistakes,
e descobrir mistérios descabidos,
intricados, rentes e quentes,
and to discover ridiculous, intricate
mysteries, hot and close,

e tomar e dar gozos em pleno gozo
das faculdades mentais,
and to give and take pleasure here, now
while we are, still, of sound mind.

In other words to listen
to the sound of the light
in the last raindrop as it slips
from leaf to roof tile, from fingertip
to aging lip, and then to taste it fully,
dizzy with glee and grief.

O DESTINO
THE DESTINATION

Transitions are not *a minha força,* my strength,
um fato um pouco louco, a kind of crazy fact
for someone who has made so many—
and has, *ainda, ainda, ainda,*
the largest one yet ahead.
Our trouble is, whatever our intentions,
we travel heavy. We carry so little of value—
clothes, blank paper, needle-nose pliers,
dried ferns, herbs, flash disks, earrings, poems
in progress—and still our bags flaunt red
warning labels. Shamed, helpless, we haul them
through the world at large, straining backs, tearing tendons,
our own, our intimates, and those of total strangers.
Decepcionado is what they use here for
disappointed. *Decepcionado comigo mesmo,* myself.
For the trouble is we travel heavy knowing full well
that sooner than justice, later than mercy,
the wind will toss us—a shower of ash
only slightly denser than mist, a lover's cry—
back into our children's eyes.

RECOMPOR

TO RESET

Em frente
Dead Ahead

Em frente! Em frente!
Whenever we ask, that's what we're told,
a hand tossed impatiently out ahead,
and we nod, reluctantly plod on,
em frente, em frente,
aware we were asking for something
vivid, seductive, *sedutor,*
misterioso, and true, not this
steadfast, plain and unprepossessing city
sem, it seems, imagination or dream.
E completamente satisfeita com si mesma.
Só. Just so.

We look virtuously right and left
and nothing lifts—not the grim cloud cover,
the indecipherable hum of a world in which
nós não queremos envolver-nos, we don't want
to get involved, and yet into which we
find ourselves *mergulhados,* plunged,
our carefree dreams *um fardo* now,
a burden, heavy as a parachute
with no ripcord.

A SAUDADE
PINING

i
A saudade . . .
There's something in the word, just
the sound of it, that gets my goat.
The savage strength of loss softened to a simple
a respiração, not these words—
longing, pining, yearning—
which still catch in the back of our throats,
whine a little, but *a saudade,*
a gauze scarf drifting,
beautiful, aimless, in a light wind.
It fits with a language that forbids
a consonant to have the final say,
that doesn't rejoice in the plosive, the fricative.
Consonant becomes *a consoante,*
purposeful, *resoluta,* construct, *idealizar.*

ii
The voice in my dreams is warm, wise,
safe as a mother's embrace, irrefutable:
*You've come here to live into the reality
of your own mortality.* The lilt of the words
eases me, and then I catch myself,
the euphony here is so contagious.
Death. We're talking about death.
Something hard as a hand knocking wood,
loud as the clang of bedpans, sharp as a scalpel
incising my freckled skin.

iii
My organs have begun to fail me
(I'm at that age), beginning with the leaf-
shaped one nuzzled in with lung
and heart just under my breast bone.
Na verdade, I can't take this idea
into the drive that defines me,
that mantra absorbed in my twenties,
so filled with grit and plosives:
"Produce! Produce!
Were it but the pitifullest,
infinitesimal fraction of a product . . .
for the night cometh wherein no man
can work." But *na verdade*, woman or man,
it is exactly here, where we're driven by fear
of that indifferent dark, driven deep inside
our life's work, that we learn
over and over and over again—
through the restless gesture emerging from clay,
the truth of a wild analogy,
or the sweet release of giving ourselves over
to a story large enough to hold us—
that, *na verdade, a arte é*
a saudade.

iv
Mortalidade também is death with
a saudade in it, something *macia,*
soft, *resplandecente,* resplendent, and
filled with passion, *cheia de paixão.*
In truth, it can grow on you, this way
of living, dying. There's something large
and timeless at its center,
and something both delicate
and *firme,* substantial, there as well,
like the pressure of resting shoulder to shoulder
with a husband of forty years, watching waves
batter the blinding sand and knowing—
his bones and mind a meteor shower
of cancer—this pleasure can't last the summer.
A saudade, to know only now—not too
late, but so very close—that this love,
so often and so bitterly disparaged
is *bastante,* more
than enough,
and always has been.

v
And there is *a saudade também*
in the gruff reminder a mother gives
her grieving children, "Remember
the one who's sickest isn't always the first to go."
And in how she sets her hands on her husband's arms,
once so generous, wasting now to bone,
and *a saudade* too in how his eyes close,
both of them knowing that the power that flows
through her comes from worlds before and after
and that she would never dream of keeping it
to herself.

vi
Na verdade, estamos louco de saudade,
we're crazy with our yearning
and with our dying, *tão cheia*
with time and *a eternidade,*
with innumerable pleasures,
and irrevocable mistakes.

Uma brecha
A Breech

Chuvosa, chorosa, rainy, tearful,
we're not *ombro a ombro*, shoulder
to shoulder, the day and I,
we're *entreolhando-nos,* eyeing
each other like a woman of two minds,
a single visage. Why have we come so far
only to home in on what we wanted
to escape in the first place?

Essa é a minha verdade pessoal e esmagadora,
this my personal and overwhelming truth:
I never want to waste another day of my life.
Just the idea that I might wakes me
like the maddening inescapable din
of the men drinking below in the corner bar,
and makes me want to roar, *bramir,*
espatifar, smash, *e esparramar,* scatter
with equal bravura the men and inner djinn.

Instead I listen for the silence *breve*
e enorme that surrounds every note
of the music ringing inside my head.
To shape and to resign oneself are the same
word here: *conformar.* The artist in me,

half mad with loneliness, *destimida,* fearless,
e capaz, delights in this *como uma outra verdade
pessoal e esmagadora.* It's true: when I leave
this world I want to leave a luminous,
lasting body of work, one that has
shaped me as want shapes waste,
and silence shapes all sound.

Recompor
To Reset

A little sun and our spirits dutifully
fizz like recapped seltzer. It's both
a gift and *uma fraqueza,* a weakness,
this resonance with the elements,
a luz do sol, sunlight, *a chuva,* rain,
a algazarra da rua, the racket
on the streets, and that one voice,
drunken, *borbulhando,* bubbling—
in tune—in the bleak echo chamber
that is *Rua das Flores* on a wet Sunday night.

I dream of the blanched flamingoes
seining algae from the fetid ponds.
This is, we concede, in wry *a auto-preservação,*
self-protection, and *a auto-comiseração,* self-pity,
a dull, dull city. No use pretending otherwise.
But there are so many ways here to translate
that thud of a word—dull—all transitive.
Diminuir (to dull pleasure).
Enfraquecer (to dull senses).
Embaciar (to dull light).

Just what moves what, that's the question.
We've seen it in so many places—the people,
the cities, the countries with no interest in
os outros, others. But what an umbrella of a word,
uma palavra guarda-chuva, Others, when
what we truly mean is us. Just us.

However self-possessed, *donos de nós mesmos*
we may think we are, it's going to happen,
after the tenth, the fiftieth, the one thousandth
indifferent gaze, we will return it, we
diminuimos, enfraquecemos, embaciamos them—
and then stop, appalled. After all, it's our own
world we're dimming, dulling, selling short
and with that *compreensão*, we return to ourselves—
porous, curious, *frágeis, ferozes, e férteis,*
fragile, fierce, fertile,
and again we look for those same gifts
in the first, fifth, and fiftieth
new and illumined face we meet,
guardando chuva, guardando sol,
like us all, like us all.

Resplandecente
Resplendent

Ruim. Vile, wicked, useless, rotten, faulty,
poor. *Ruins.* The plural. *O pensamento ruim.*
Bad thought. *Os pensamentos ruins.*
Just more of the same. Drop it!
Deixar pra lá! Oh don't I wish—just
to do it, just to stop questioning what no longer
needs questioning—*identidade*, purpose, plot—
and just questing. But where? For what?
Despite myself I've grown fond
of the hubbub on the cobbled pedestrian way,
the pulse of the hawkers, the thrum
of dreams I can't find my way into,
they're so intimate and unself-conscious.
Fond too of this quirky skyline, its drab concrete
high-rises, church steeples, corrugated rooftops,
and the oblique angle at which I view
the silvered dome glinting above four baroque clocks,
each boldly facing up to a cardinal direction,
none keeping exactly the same time,
and all differing from mine. *Na verdade,*
fond frees me to leave. *Então,*
amanhã à noite, so tomorrow
night, we *rumamos,*
head out for somewhere new
inside us, *resplandecentamente*
ordinary.

NO MEIO DESTE

IN THE THICK OF THIS

No meio deste
In the Thick of This

I wake crying, the whole room an echo chamber
of the life on the street. I can't hear myself think.
The language out there remains pure rhythm, plaint.
I can't escape. I too *estou na rua,* a Skid Row bum.
I'm right there, lost deep in God's eardrum,
no centro do tímpano da Diosa, muddled by roars and yelps,
incomprehensible jokes, *as ironías,* ironies both
bitter and kind, *amargas e amáveis,* and the shudder
and groan of garbage trucks and lost intentions
both *bem e mal.* How in the hell have I gotten here,
to this caesura—or raw fissure—
between time and sense? The words will never
se tornarão claras, come clear, come clean
and it matters, it really matters.
Estou na rua. I'm out on the street.
Estou presa. I'm stuck.
Importa. Não importa.
What matters is what carries over,
carries *us* over from one world to the next.

Because in infancy words caught in my throat
or madly shaken out almost proved
the death of me, they became
my raison d'être, terra firma, dura mata,
my through-thick-and-thin skin.
But here, *não importa.* It all comes pouring
meaninglessly in. *Estou na rua.*

Sou sem-teto. Homeless. I'm a distant echo
no tímpano da Diosa. Na verdade, notwithstanding,
eu sou. I am. *Sou. E sou semelhante,* I'm twinned
with the woman who without warning lifted her head
out of the tropical leaves in the park at three
on Sunday afternoon, then slipped back down
onto her cardboard carpet, rose again like Venus
from her undulant sea of green, combing
with dusty fingers, *penteando com seus dedos
empoeirados,* a thicket of russet hair—
a gesture so sensuous and brazenly generous
it still sings in my own body and mind,
uma potência, um sinal, a power, a sign.

Apoiou
Supported

You crow when you find it, the word
that confirms our deepest suspicions—
that this language truly is on the verge
of dissolving completely into vowels:
It's easy enough to sing, a-p-o-i-o-u,
but just how should we convert it
to the rapid slur of daily speech?
A-pó-joo. So close in sound to *apogeu*,
the crowning point, our apogee,
and still it sounds so oppositional.
Third person. Singular. Past. *Ele* or *ela
se apoiou*. They did. They helped.
For no reason, no reason at all.
It gives me pause. I oppose the thought
for it doesn't include us. City after city,
it never does. I'm so turned off these days
by my surroundings, but the tawdriness
of this city is not so very different
from our own. It's *uma cidade normal*—
with its dog shit and broken glass
and ubiquitous graffiti: *o imperialismo
é um tigre de papel,* imperialism is just,
don't we all know it, a paper tiger.
Here, the small shops are as sparsely stocked
as any country store or ghetto market in Georgia.
And, like there, the shelves, half-bare, still hold

the essentials: *o pão,* bread, *o sabão,* soap, *o queijo,* cheese,
o molho de tomate, tomato sauce, *a água mineral,*
bottled water, and *as velas,* candles
for when the lights go out—
so it's not so different, not so different at all.
This homely insight *me apoiou,* just like this pun.
The ground, today, *me apoiou.* Life itself
more times than I can count *me apoiou.*
And who knows, even here, one day *um homen
ou uma mulher* (still yet to be met),
me apoiaria, and I too may come to the aid
of a total stranger, *o apoiaria,*
for no reason, no reason at all.

Os anseios e os pertences
Longings and Belongings

A man howls on the street
in the middle of the day,
in pure and simple
fúria, fury,
e raiva, rage.
He has lost his bearings,
here in Porto Alegre,
on a sunny *sábado* in May,
but the sound seems to swell
from my own soul. I'm waiting
to see if someone claims him
although I already know
I understand him as well,
perhaps better, than anyone else here.
This sound *pertence a mim,*
belongs to me. Exactly.
I find it ravishing.

The only thing traveling teaches me
is that we all live within
amazingly small compasses,
a house, a family circle,
a city block, an itinerary,
a campfire, an igloo, a scream.
Wherever we are, we mark our territory
like dogs, we string lines from one pole

of our being to the other, and hang out
to dry our precious belongings,
ragged or new. He wears no shoes
but strides inside his sound, *o seu som*,
from here to kingdom come, gripping
the straps of his knapsack and,
if only he knew, carrying me too,
in all my poverty, *a minha penúria,*
and my fullness, *a minha plenitude,*
of spirit. As he turns the corner
without looking back, I cling,
if only he knew, closer to him
than his own shadow.

Abandonando as suposições
Abandoning Assumptions

In the absence of evidence to the contrary,
I assume the world will do just as well
without me. But on this sunny morning
in Porto Alegre as I keep distant vigil
for a father who insisted, perhaps still
mutely insists, to ghosts vengeful and
forgiving, living and dead, on the value,
the inestimable value of his own
continued existence, I ponder my own
assumption, *a minha suposição,*
the profligate waste of it.

Na flor da minha idade, na minha plenitude,
in the flower of my own age, my own
plenitude, I reconsider this assumption
tão inconsciente, unconscious, core.
For *na verdade*, in truth, I have received
and receive now more love than I
could ever or can even now
imagine, *mas ainda assim,*
nonetheless, I live as if abandonment,
o abandono, e só e somente o abandono,
were my only truth.

But *hoje*, today, *senti,* I felt my father
a continent away, so close to death
and the powers that be he rarely
wakes, stirring restlessly in his bed
and still pleading, as he always has,
to go on at any cost. And I understood,
comprendi, what it really means
to let go of what has shaped us
most completely and that
it will cost me just as much to abandon
a minha suposição as it will *o meu pai,*
my father, to abandon his. *Comprendi
e comprendo,* I got it and I still get it,
I really get why he still wrangles so stubbornly
with his own remorseless angels, why he would
rather die than give it up, *a sua suposição,
muitas vezes mais nua e crua* than mine—
for anything, *mesmo graça,* even grace.

E sinto, sinto muito,
I'm sorry, I'm so sorry
for both of us.

Os haveres
Belongings

Haver isn't, in Portuguese, the all purpose auxiliary,
but persists, impersonal and blessing, and its synonyms,
to exist, to have a place, to be in time,
are, *na verdade,* more necessary *para o meu espírito,*
so prescient and *impermanente* these days.

Há—there is, there just is—
*a credibilidade, a ternura, o poder,
e o azar,* credibility, tenderness,
power and luck.

E havia—and there has been,
there just has been—so much
that has been less than death
and so much that *haverá,* will be,
more than life. Repeatedly.

And then, *há,* there is, there just is
a husband who rests his head in my arms
and sighs *com luxúria* and I know
I am home and homecoming to him,
mutuamente. Eu!, so prescient and *impermanente,
sou,* am, *era,* have been, and *serei,* will be,
um milagre humano to him, as he is to me.
Há. Ah! *Mutuamente.*

Na marra
In Full Strength, Overwhelmingly

My father appears on my computer screen
in real time, frail, eyelids quivering,
a minha raposa manhosa, my sly fox,
close to comatose—and I am
despite myself *invado na marra,*
overcome by all that he is now,
almost dumb, deaf, and blind.

Astonished at myself, I fight
por este homen, this man who chose,
more times than chance can claim,
to betray, deceive, and undermine,
and *faz nas coxas,* make a fucking bollocks
of his private life. And this
is what is left, his sparse hair
flaring in the light, his body
fetal, his cough opening
his soul to eternity.

Perhaps he hears me
assuring him that what he has done
his best to create, evade, desecrate,
a sua sentença eterna, his final judgment,
ends here in these rooms. *The good,*
I whisper, *will outlive you.* It is a curse
and a blessing and the best I can do.

Across the street, a stranger peers
from his balcony, the old concrete
is blackened, faintly European
in its seediness, as real
as my own breath *que abre*
a minha alma, opens my own soul
to the full weight of this sorrow
so bearable, *decisivo,* and
inexplicably simple:
Because you were, we are.

And we are the best of you, a truth
that grips and shapes us all now
just like your lies used to.
Na marra.
Na marra.
Na marra.

Cabal
Complete, Utter, Ultimate

Each morning on the beach, I find, nested
like eggs in sand bowls, *as oferendas,* offerings
to the many gods who survived the dark passage
and thrive here. *Os charutos,* cigars, half-smoked.
Candles. Long-stemmed roses, *as rosas,*
brancas, white, *e vermelhas,* red. Gold
chrysanthemums. A white cake iced with ants.
A toppled plastic champagne flute. *E hoje,*
just for me, tossing and turning in the surf,
another offering, a small blue boat, *um barco azul,*
which floated away *e voltou,* washed back, so many times
and so tantalizingly close, I knew
it was destined for me. Crudely made, it's both
o lixo, trash, and *o tesouro inestimável,* priceless treasure.
It's *o meu direito de passagem,* my right of way,
and my rite of *a travessia,* sea passage, too.
What prayers did it ferry out to sea?
E que onda, which wave sent it back
to tempt me?

Here, *está tudo azul,* everything is blue,
means everything is rosy, and that's just how I feel,
in this land where what we toss away and what
just floats off are indistinguishable,
they're *ambos,* both, just *o entulho,* debris.

Foam whirls around my ankles as I bend to claim
what has already claimed me, this washing
out and in and out and in and out and in,
este ritmo impecável, impeccable, and gloriously
haphazard, that fits me as well, *o que me cai tão bem
nas roupas da imperatriz,* the empress's new clothes.

Or the wind and water that soon will shroud
the ashes of my father.

HOME

EM CASA

Em casa
Home

i
When heard, it is so silent and so sure,
essa língua de nossos orgãos, this language
of our viscera, that we believe we need
no more words. It *knows* us, whole,
and death too, and restlessness and the sweet
sure flow of a lifetime. Impossible to disown—
but it holds inner whirlwinds, *os redemoinhos,* too,
and *os furações,* cyclones, *os precipícios
e as pragas,* cliffs and plagues,
também. Just listen.

ii
Like nitroglycerin tablets just ready
to slip under our tongues, that's how we carry
back this Portuguese and the unexpected
alternatives it provides. It distinguishes between
forms of release: from captivity, *libertação,*
from pain, *liberação.* And forms of belonging:
pertencer a alguém, be someone's property,
ou fazer parte, be a member,
ou encaixar-se, just fit. To disown is
renegar and when we bring it back into our lives,
slip it under our native tongue, it reminds us
when hearts ache, tears burn, blood
chills, and words are swallowed back,
that promises were once made, then broken.

iii
Estava renegada. Eu! Too. Honestly,
it shocks me and that shocks me even more.
I am, however I want to try to deny it,
taken aback by the simple act of taking back
what was never asked for but promised
all the same, what it might mean to truly be
uma renegada. Eu! Just asking in that way
makes a home for what is most unspeakable
and *desejável,* desirable, in me. So, I'm
uma renegada, a renegade, at my age.
For I too can choose to recant, forswear, deny
various understandings, choose among synonyms
what best describes this act of taking back that so haunts
my own younger brother and sister. Did my father,
when he was so frail, so afraid of dying, still so
terminally sly, deny, abnegate, disavow,
recant, forswear, or just tergiversate when he
secretly *renegou* the equality he had so often
and so publicly claimed for all his children?

iv
To need in Portuguese is *precisar*.
I love its precision. *Preciso*.
I need. *Não preciso*. I don't need.
Fiz isso sem precisar. I did this
without needing to. Yes, I did.
I never needed to pretend, as I have
so ably and so long, that a promise wasn't made,
accepted, and betrayed. To be confused,
disoriented, is *desnortear*. So these days,
on this side of the equator,
I look for the North Star
where I'm sure it can be found
and I ponder: *A quem eu pertenço?*
Who do I belong to?
Do que eu faço parte? What am I part of?
Onde eu me encaixo? Where do I fit?

v
Each question is an answer, *uma liberação
da dor*, a release from pain, and
I hoard it, take it into a quiet deeper
than I've ever known before,
into a *silêncio orgânico*, which already holds
so much, as yet another unsung hymn
ready to soar—and equally content
to wait, speechless, savoring its strength.

Ficar a Mercê das Cigarras e da Misericórdia
To Be at the Mercy of Cicadas and Compassion

Suddenly we're aware it's here, the song
of the cicadas and are amazed
by how it burrows so immediately
and so straight into the heart
of summer and into our hearts too—
and then expands into voids,
wounds whose existence we've refused
to admit. *Cheio.* Full. *O nosso mundo
está cheio agora.* Our world is full now.
Mas cheio do que? But full of what?
It would be ok with me
if it were just this sound, just this surging
and falling back, this miraculous
bouyance and embrace,
transbordando, overflowing,
but it also, like the sea, *derruba,*
overthrows and ruthlessly debrides
what can't *renovar ou renascer,*
renew or spring up again
even with our help, our hope.
And that hurts. There are stories
in each of us that fester, eat away
at what's most essential in us, *repele,*
repel all our best efforts to heal.
There are words that can't be unsaid, acts
that can't be taken back, denied, or repaired, whole

systems that will never flourish and never
let us loose. That's the god awful, god rueful
truth—and so is this sound that reaches
sem aviso, without warning, into those same depths,
so fresh, raging with something purer and more primal
than joy, and sure, so sure, of its welcome.

ACKNOWLEDGEMENTS

Thanks to our teachers Ana Carolina and Rosane at The Language Club in Florianópolis for so gently and warmly introducing us to Portuguese and to Tatiana Wiedmann, also in Florianópolis, for so meticulously and sensitively editing the Portuguese in this manuscript several years later. Any errors that remain are mine.

Thanks as well to Kathleen Housley for her careful reading of this work in manuscript, to the other members of the Wising Up Writers Collective for their early interest and support, and to Charles Brockett, *meu velhinho*, who has adventured with me into so many new places, new languages.

In the companion recording, I want to gratefully acknowledge, and lightly evoke in the brief interstices between poems, the pervasive influence of ambient sound on my experiences of Brazil, especially the music—of street performers and protesters heard in passing, the waves, the wind, the rain, the raucous traffic, the often incomprehensible murmur of human voices, as well as the sea swell of cicadas and the riffs of birds on my return.

HEATHER TOSTESON, a writer and visual artist, is the author of *The Sanctity of the Moment: Poems from Four Decades*, *Germs of Truth*, *Visible Signs*, *Hearts as Big as Fists & Other Stories*, and *God Speaks My Language, Can You?* She has received a Nation/Discovery prize for her poetry and fellowships for poetry, fiction, and photography from MacDowell, Yaddo, VCCA and Hambidge. She holds an MFA in Creative Writing (UNC-Greensboro) and PhD in English and Creative Writing (Ohio University).

www.ingramcontent.com/pod-product-compliance
Lightning Source LLC
Chambersburg PA
CBHW022121090426
42743CB00008B/943